T0137602

TRANSCENDENTAL FIRE

KIMBRA FISHEL

Copyright © 2016 Kimbra Fishel.

All rights reserved. No part of this book may be used or reproduced by any means, graphic, electronic, or mechanical, including photocopying, recording, taping or by any information storage retrieval system without the written permission of the author except in the case of brief quotations embodied in critical articles and reviews.

WestBow Press books may be ordered through booksellers or by contacting:

WestBow Press
A Division of Thomas Nelson & Zondervan
1663 Liberty Drive
Bloomington, IN 47403
www.westbowpress.com
1 (866) 928-1240

Because of the dynamic nature of the Internet, any web addresses or links contained in this book may have changed since publication and may no longer be valid. The views expressed in this work are solely those of the author and do not necessarily reflect the views of the publisher, and the publisher hereby disclaims any responsibility for them.

Any people depicted in stock imagery provided by Thinkstock are models, and such images are being used for illustrative purposes only. Certain stock imagery © Thinkstock.

This book is a work of non-fiction. Unless otherwise noted, the author and the publisher make no explicit guarantees as to the accuracy of the information contained in this book and in some cases, names of people and places have been altered to protect their privacy.

Scripture taken from the King James Version of the Bible.

ISBN: 978-1-5127-2533-9 (sc)
ISBN: 978-1-5127-2534-6 (e)

Library of Congress Control Number: 2015921454

Print information available on the last page.

WestBow Press rev. date: 1/7/2016

FOREWORD

Each day is a fresh, unpredictable display of beauty here on the southern Great Plains. I consider this creative gift to be God's concession for the blazing hot summer days and the icy wintery blasts we must endure. Miniscule drops of mist kiss awaiting leaves. Gentle morning breezes massage slender blades of grass. Tree limbs begin to flex and stretch in anticipation of nature's aerobic workout which surely will follow when the winds come sweeping down the plains. But all else pales in the presence of panoramic horizons which become the canvas for unspeakable beauty by day and by night. Ever-changing colors, both subtle and brilliant, entertain anyone who will simply look up.

Zedekiah, king of ancient Judah, asked the prophet Jeremiah, "Is there any word from the LORD?" (Jeremiah 31:17, KJV) The question reminds me of King David's memorable song, "The heavens declare the glory of God; and the firmament sheweth his handiwork. Day unto day uttereth speech, and night unto night sheweth knowledge. There is no speech nor language, where their voice is not heard." (Psalm 19:1-3, KJV) As surely as God spoke through ancient prophets and his son, Jesus Christ, God is carrying on a conversation with humankind through the beauty and glory of his creative handiwork.

Kimbra Fishel has combined her photographic gifts with her deep devotion to God to offer this beautiful collection. The interweaving of a creative eye and a heart that is attuned to Holy Scripture result in a volume which will both inspire and teach any of us who will simply take a moment and witness the glories which daily grace each of us without respect to our station in life. To God be the glory.

Jim Shepherd

Pastor, Goodrich Memorial United Methodist Church of Norman, OK

INTRODUCTION

God's majestic creation is on display for all to see. I am privileged to capture these images. From beautiful sunrises to glorious sunsets, from the threatening of storm clouds to the mysteries of space, these photos reflect a snapshot in time. Gone forever is that exact moment of specific whirling colors, detailed contrasts and beams of light. I stand in awe each day, wondering what sights I will behold. God's incredible wonders reflect an even greater reality; that we live in an unfolding story. It is a story filled with miracles and majesty, darkness and despair. It is a story in which the ending is known, yet the details of how we arrive are obscured. It is a story of Good versus Evil. It is a story of Love conquering all while tempered with righteousness and holiness. It is a story of fall and redemption, of sacrifice and victory. It is a story of free will and choice, the most important choice we will ever make; for it is a story of eternity. If you are wandering lost, wondering which way to go, return to the Word. Live the Word. Breathe the Word. See the Word in all Creation.

Return to the beginning….

In the beginning was the Word, and the Word was with God, and the Word was God. The same was in the beginning with God. All things were made by him; and without him was not any thing made that was made. In him was life; and the life was the light of men. And the light shineth in darkness; and the darkness comprehended it not.

John 1: 1-5

And God said, Let there be lights in the firmament of the heaven to divide the day from the night; and let them be for signs, and for seasons, and for days, and years

Genesis 1:14

*Thine, O L*ORD *is the greatness, and the power, and the glory, and the victory, and the majesty: for all that is in the heaven and in the earth is thine; thine is the kingdom, O L*ORD, *and thou art exalted as head above all.*

Chronicles 29:11

Shall mortal man be more just than God? Shall a man be more pure than his maker? Behold, he put no trust in his servants; and his angels he charged with folly: How much less in them that dwell in houses of clay, whose foundation is in the dust, which are crushed before the moth?

Job 4:17-29

Woe to the rebellious children, saith the Lord, that take counsel, but not of me; and that cover with a covering, but not of my spirit, that they may add sin to sin:

Isaiah 30:1

Therefore, the Lord himself
shall give you a sign; Behold
a virgin shall conceive, and
bear a son, and shall call his
name Immanuel.

Isaiah 7:14

And, behold, thou shalt conceive in thy womb, and bring forth a son, and shalt call his name JESUS.

Luke 1:31

For unto you is born this day in the city of David a Saviour, which is Christ the Lord.

Luke 2:11

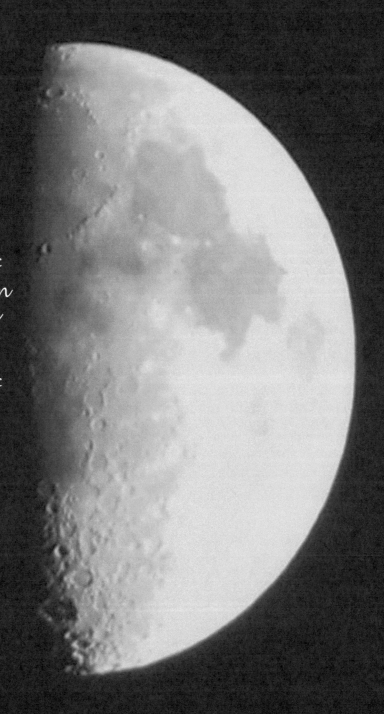

When I consider thy
heavens, the work of
thy fingers, the moon
and the stars, which
thou hast ordained
What is man, that
thou art mindful of
him? and the son
of man, that thou
visitest him?

Psalm 8: 3-4

The voice of the Lord is upon the waters: the God of glory thundereth: the Lord is upon many waters. The voice of the Lord is powerful; the voice of the Lord is full of majesty.

Psalm 29:3-4

And lead us not into temptation, but deliver us from evil: For thine is the kingdom, and the power, and the glory, for ever. Amen.

Matthew 6:13

Peace I leave with you, my peace I give unto you: not as the world giveth, give I unto you. Let not your heart be troubled, neither let it be afraid.

John 14:27

Yet the Lord will command his lovingkindness in the day time, and in the night his song shall be with me, and my prayer unto the God of my life.

Psalm 42:8

For God so loved the world, that he gave his only begotten Son, that whosoever believeth in him should not perish, but have everlasting life. For God sent not his Son into the world to condemn the world; but that the world through him might be saved. He that believeth on him is not condemned: but he that believeth not is condemned already, because he hath not believed in the name of the only begotten Son of God. And this is the condemnation, that light is come into the world, and men loved darkness rather than light, because their deeds were evil.

John 3:16-19

Thou art the God that doest wonders: thou hast declared thy strength among the people.

Psalm 77:14

For God, who commanded the light to shine out of darkness, hath shined in our hearts, to give the light of the knowledge of the glory of God in the face of Jesus Christ.

2 Corinthians 4:6

Blessed be the Lord God, the God of Israel, who only doeth wondrous things.

Psalm 72:18

But he was wounded for our transgressions, he was bruised for our iniquities: the chastisement of our peace was upon him; and with his stripes we are healed.

Isaiah 53:5

Then the eleven disciples went away into Galilee, into a mountain where Jesus had appointed them. And when they saw him, they worshipped him: but some doubted. And Jesus came and spake unto them, saying, All power is given unto me in heaven and in earth. Go ye therefore, and teach all nations, baptizing them in the name of the Father, and of the Son, and of the Holy Ghost: Teaching them to observe all things whatsoever I have commanded you: and, lo, I am with you always, even unto the end of the world. Amen.

Matthew 28:16-20

Wherefore we receiving a kingdom which cannot be moved, let us have grace, whereby we may serve God acceptably with reverence and godly fear: For our God is a consuming fire.

Hebrews 12:28-29

For now we see through a glass, darkly; but then face to face: now I know in part; but then shall I know even as also I am known.

1 Corinthians 13:12

And it shall come to pass afterward, that I will pour out my spirit upon all flesh; and your sons and your daughters shall prophesy, your old men shall dream dreams, your young men shall see visions: And also upon the servants and upon the handmaids in those days will I pour out my spirit.

Joel 2:28-29

Howbeit when he, the Spirit of truth, is come, he will guide you into all truth: for he shall not speak of himself; but whatsoever he shall hear, that shall he speak: and he will shew you things to come.

John 16:13

Cause me to hear thy lovingkindness in the morning; for in thee do I trust: cause me to know the way wherein I should walk; for I lift up my soul unto thee.

Psalm 143:8

Behold, I shew you a mystery; We shall not all sleep, but we shall all be changed, In a moment, in the twinkling of an eye, at the last trump: for the trumpet shall sound, and the dead shall be raised incorruptible, and we shall be changed.

1 Corinthians 15:51-52

I have remembered thy name, O Lᴏʀᴅ, in the night, and have kept thy law.

Psalm 119:55

For yourselves know perfectly that the day of the Lord so cometh as a thief in the night. For when they shall say, Peace and safety; then sudden destruction cometh upon them, as travail upon a woman with child; and they shall not escape. But ye, brethren, are not in darkness, that that day should overtake you as a thief. Ye are all the children of light, and the children of the day: we are not of the night, nor of darkness. Therefore let us not sleep, as do others; but let us watch and be sober.

Thessalonians 5:2-6

Trust in the Lord with all thine heart; and lean not unto thine own understanding. In all thy ways acknowledge him, and he shall direct thy paths.

Proverbs 3:5-6

For there is nothing covered, that shall not be revealed; neither hid, that shall not be known.

Luke 12:2

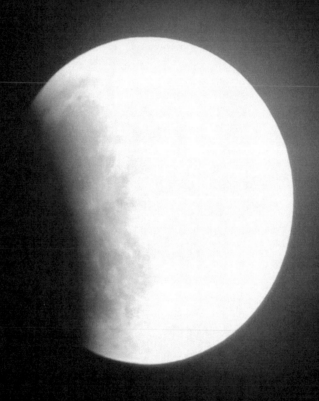

And I will shew wonders in heaven above, and signs in the earth beneath; blood, and fire, and vapour of smoke:

Acts 2:19

My sheep hear my voice, and I know them, and they follow me: And I give unto them eternal life; and they shall never perish, neither shall any man pluck them out of my hand. My Father, which gave them me, is greater than all; and no man is able to pluck them out of my Father's hand. I and my Father are one.

John 10:27-30

The sun shall be turned into darkness, and the moon into blood,
before the great and terrible day of the Lord come.

Joel 2:31

The grass withereth, the flower fadeth: but the word of our God shall stand for ever.

Isaiah 40:8

For it is written, As I live, saith the Lord, every knee shall bow to me, and every tongue shall confess to God.

Romans 14:11

Submit yourselves therefore to God, resist the devil, and he will flee from you.

James 4:7

Behold, he cometh with clouds; and every eye shall see him, and they also which pierced him: and all kindred of the earth shall wail because of him...I am Alpha and Omega, the beginning and the ending, saith the Lord, which is, and which was, and which is to come, the Almighty.

Revelation 1:7,8

And I saw, and behold a white
horse: and he that sat on him
had a bow; and a crown was
given unto him: and he went
forth conquering, and to conquer.

Revelation 6:2

For, behold, I create new heavens and a new earth: and the former shall not be remembered, nor come into mind.

Isaiah 65:17

And there shall be no night there; and they need no candle, neither light of the sun; for the Lord God giveth them light: and they shall reign for ever and ever.

Revelation 22:5

Behold, I come quickly: blessed is he that keepeth the sayings of the prophecy of this book.

Revelation 22:7

AFTERWORD

My heart is overwhelmed. As children, Kim and I grew up having fun and enjoying life. It was wonderful, but something was missing. I believed in God and she did not. Sometimes my heart was heavy and tears were shed because I was concerned about my friend. I wanted her to be in Heaven with me. Years later, seemingly out of the blue, Kim told me about a Voice she had heard. I was hoping this was the answer to my prayer but was not sure until I received an e-mail from her saying that she and her daughter were baptized! What a glorious day that was! Now we have such a wonderful connection and can share such a wonderful Savior!

As God revealed His Word and Works to Kim, she felt a calling to record His feats of nature. In so doing Kim's love for photography increased, and her beautiful work artistically portrays the wondrous masterpieces of our Father! The addition of scripture sends chills through me as I ponder what God says through this marvelous gift He has given to my dear friend. I praise God for all that He is doing through Kim, and I know that everyone who experiences this book will feel His Presence! All glory and honor to God!

Kathy Barnes, Pastor

Open Arms Fellowship

Tulsa, Oklahoma

Printed in the United States
By Bookmasters